T0017104

Joyful Books for Curious Minds

An imprint of Macmillan Children's Publishing Group, LLC
Odd Dot ® is a registered trademark of Macmillan Publishing Group, LLC.
120 Broadway, New York, NY 10271
OddDot.com • mackids.com

Copyright © 2024 by Odd Dot
All rights reserved.

EDITOR Nathalie Le Du
DESIGNER Christina Quintero
PRODUCTION EDITOR Mia Moran
PRODUCTION MANAGER Jocelyn O'Dowd

Library of Congress Control Number: 2023040537

ISBN 978-1-250-34889-0

Our books are available at special discounts when purchased in bulk for premiums and sales promotions as well as for fund-raising or educational use. Special editions or book excerpts also can be created to specification. For details, contact the Macmillan Corporate and Premium Sales Department at (800) 221-7945 ext. 5442, or send an email to MacmillanSpecialMarkets@macmillan.com.

This work is an independent biography and is not authorized, sponsored, or endorsed by Taylor Swift.

First edition, 2024

Printed in the United States of America by Worzalla, Stevens Point, Wisconsin

1 3 5 7 9 10 8 6 4 2

A Book for the Littlest Taylor Swift Fans

You Are Fearless

illustrated by Laura Catrinella

New York

You are . . .
fearless, baby,

an original who cannot be copied.

You make . . . the world pay attention,

besties come together,

You create . . .
power from pain,

courage from kindness,

friends from strangers.

A trailblazer of change,

an inspiration who never goes out of style.

You exceed my wildest dreams, baby!

And your era
has just begun.